World Records to Wow You!

by Grace Hansen

ABDO
SEEING IS BELIEVING
Kids

abdopublishing.com

Published by Abdo Kids, a division of ABDO, PO Box 398166, Minneapolis, Minnesota 55439.

Printed in the United States of America, North Mankato, Minnesota.

102014

012015

THIS BOOK CONTAINS
RECYCLED MATERIALS

Photo Credits: AP Images, Getty Images, iStock, Landov Media, Shutterstock

Production Contributors: Teddy Borth, Jennie Forsberg, Grace Hansen

Design Contributors: Laura Rask, Dorothy Toth

Library of Congress Control Number: 2014943786

Cataloging-in-Publication Data

Hansen, Grace.

 World records to wow you! / Grace Hansen.

  p. cm. -- (Seeing is believing)

ISBN 978-1-62970-736-5

Includes index.

1. World records--Juvenile literature. 2. Curiosities and wonders--Juvenile literature.   I. Title.

031--dc23

2014943786

Table of Contents

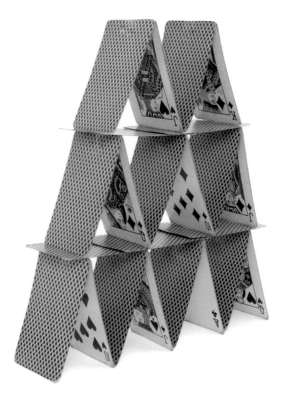

Speed

Usain Bolt is the fastest man on two legs. He is from Jamaica. He ran the 100-meter dash in 9.58 seconds.

4

Kenichi Ito is the fastest man on four legs. He is from Japan. He "ran" the 100-meter dash in 17.47 seconds.

6

Numbers

Fan Yang has held 16 records using bubbles. Once, he put an elephant inside a bubble!

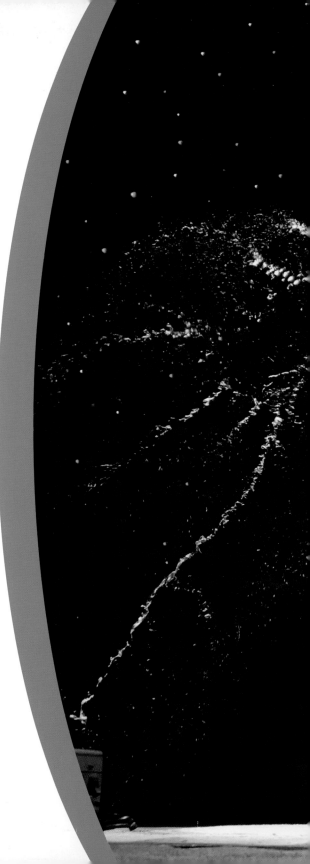

Need a superhero? There were a lot in Los Angeles on October 2, 2010. Exactly 1,580 people dressed up. That was a record.

Length & Height

The largest **3-D** street painting was over 1,000 feet (305 m) long. It was more than 24 feet (7 m) wide. It took over 20 days to paint.

Lee Redmond had the longest nails ever. Added up, they were more than 28 feet (8.5 m) long!

Bryan Berg is a **master** builder. Instead of brick, he uses cards. His tallest model was more than 25 feet (7.6 m).

17

The tallest living man is Sultan Kosen. He is 8 feet 3 inches (251 cm) tall. The shortest living man is 21.5 inches (55 cm) tall.

18

Age

Julian Pavone is the youngest **pro** drummer. He went pro at 4 years 10 months 15 days old.

More Facts

- When Sultan Kosen was named World's Tallest Man, he said his dream was to be married. In 2013, his dream came true! His suit was made from nearly 20 feet of **fabric**.

- Julian Pavone began playing drums on his father's lap at 3 months old. Born in 2004, Julian has already been on more than 300 television shows. He has worked with some of the best drummers. He also helps within his community.

- Fan Yang has put 100 people inside one soap bubble. His record was broken on March 1, 2014. Someone else put 214 people inside one soap bubble!

Glossary

3-D – short for three-dimensional.

fabric – material for making clothes and other things.

master – having very great skill.

pro – short for professional.

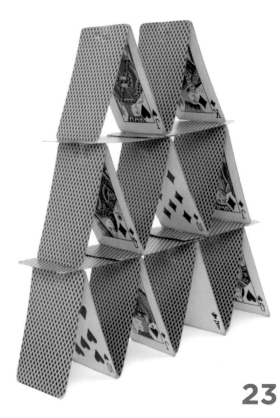

Index

abdokids.com

Use this code to log on to abdokids.com and access crafts, games, videos, and more!

Abdo Kids Code:
SWK7365